KU-616-049

START-UP SCIENCE

Wet and Dry

By Jack Challoner

Contents

Belitha Press

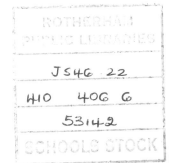

ROTHERHAM
PUBLIC LIBRARIES

J546.22

H10   406 6

53142

SCHOOLS STOCK

First published in Great Britain in 1995 by
Belitha Press Ltd
31 Newington Green
London N16 9PU

Copyright © in this format Belitha Press Ltd 1995
Text © Jack Challoner 1995

All rights reserved. No part of this book may be reproduced
or utilized in any form or by any means, electronic or
mechanical, including photocopying, recording or by any
information storage or retrieval system without permission
from the publisher except by a reviewer who
may quote brief passages in a review.

British Library Cataloguing in
Publication Data for this book
is available from the British Library.

Acknowledgements

Bubbles: 20 Ian West.
Bruce Coleman: 21 bottom Chris James.
FLPA: 11 centre Martin Withers, 13 top D P Wilson,
17 centre and 31 E & D Hosking, 18 P Berry, 19 A Wharton.
NHPA: 27 Stephen Dalton.
Oxford Scientific Films: 8 John Downer, 29 Tony Martin, 30 Eyal Bartov.
Planet Earth Pictures: 10 and 12 John Lythgoe,
13 centre G Van Ryckevorsel.
Science Photo Library: 9 top Keith Kent,
26 Dr Morley Read,
28 Sinclair Stammers.
Tony Stone Images: 11 top.
Zefa: Front Cover.

All other photographs by Claire Paxton
Thanks to models Cherelle, Hayley, Jack, Jamie, Joe, Leila and Dylan

ISBN 1-85561-396-4

Edited by Liz Harman
Designed by Hayley Cove
Illustrated by David Gifford
Picture research by Juliet Duff

Science adviser Geoff Leyland,
Head Teacher, Hady Primary School,
Chesterfield

Manufactured in China

Words in **bold** appear in the glossary on page 32.

Wet and dry

This book will answer lots of questions that you may have about wet things and dry things. But it will also make you think for yourself.

Each time you turn a page, you will find an activity that you can do yourself at home or at school. You may need help from an adult.

We all know that water is wet. When we play with water, we get wet, too. But what is water, and where does it go when we dry ourselves? How do we stay dry when it rains?

What is wet?

Water makes things wet. We use water every day to wash. Our eyes need to stay wet all the time. What things do you know that are wet?

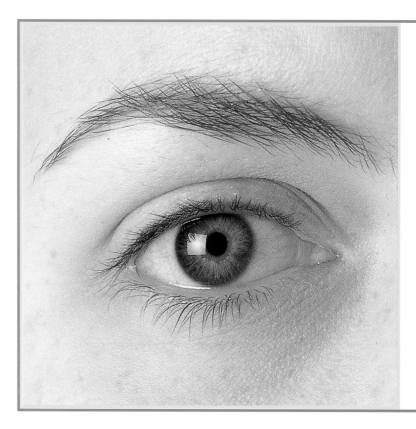

Wet eyes

Our eyes need to stay wet. A special watery mixture washes over the front of our eyes each time we blink – about 20 times every minute.

Did you know?

The smallest amount of water is called a water **molecule**. Molecules are very small. There are more of them in one drop of water than there are people in the whole world.

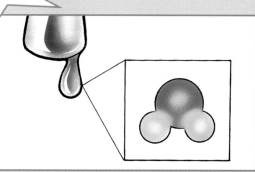

Frozen water

Snow and **ice** are wet because they are made of frozen water. When snow or ice melt, they become liquid water again.

Water for washing

How do you use water in the bathroom? This boy is washing his face with water. Where else can you see water in this picture?

Now try this

Sponges can hold large amounts of water. They are useful for washing.

You will need
A sponge, a sink full of water.

1 Soak the sponge in the water.

2 Lift it out of the water, and wait until it stops dripping.

3 Squeeze the sponge over the sink. How much water comes out?

What is dry?

What things are dry?
The clothes you are
wearing? Your hair? When
wet things become dry,
where does the water go?

Fallen leaves

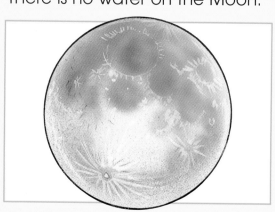

Did you know?

There is no water on the Moon.

Many trees lose their leaves
for the winter. Once a leaf
has fallen from a tree, it no
longer gets any water.
These leaves have dried
up on the forest floor.

Hot air

Some people use hair dryers to dry their hair. The warm, dry air from a hair dryer takes the water away faster than a towel.

Dry clothes

Clothes are hung up to dry after they have been washed. When they are dry, they are ready to wear.

Now try this

When it is warm, water slowly disappears. It **evaporates** to become part of the air.

You will need
Two saucers, some water, a teaspoon.

1 Put about one teaspoon of water on to each of the saucers.

2 Put one saucer somewhere warm and the other saucer in the fridge.

3 Look at the saucers every few hours. Which water dries up first?

Clouds and rain

Have you ever wondered what **clouds** are made of? Next time it rains, look at the clouds. Each cloud is made of water, and the water falls from the sky as drops of rain.

A wet day

In some parts of the world, called the **tropics**, it rains nearly every day. The rain is warm, and falls very fast.

Did you know?

The wettest places in the world have more than 11 metres of rain each year. The water runs into rivers and into the sea.

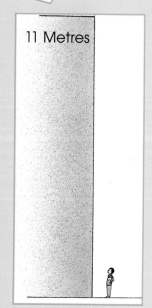

11 Metres

Dark clouds

This thundercloud is made up of tiny drops of water and ice. There is enough water in this cloud for a huge storm.

Down the drain

Water that falls on roads and paths stays there as puddles or washes away down drains like this one.

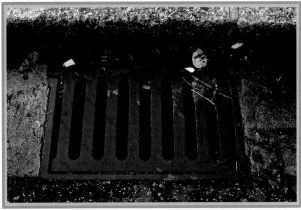

Now try this

A cloud is a mist of tiny droplets. These droplets join together to make drops which fall as rain.

You will need
A plant sprayer, a large ground floor window.

1 Stand outside the window, and make sure it is closed.

2 Make sure that the sprayer makes a fine mist. Spray water all over the window.

3 Keep spraying until drops form and run down the window.

Rain and rivers

Have you ever seen a river? Much of the water that falls as rain finds its way to rivers. What happens to a river if there is not enough rain, or if there is too much rain?

Did you know?

Water joins a river all the way along, but each river has a place where it starts. This place is called its **source**. The sources of most rivers are in mountains.

Dried-up river

Many people use the water in rivers for washing, cooking and for fun. But when there is not enough rain to keep a river full of water, the river can dry up.

Flooded river

When too much rain falls, it can make a river flood. People living near a river have to move away because water from the river floods their homes.

River banks

The sides of a river are called its banks. River banks are home for many plants and animals, which depend on the river water.

Now try this

Water always flows downhill. Where a river bends, the water moves from side to side, or **meanders**.

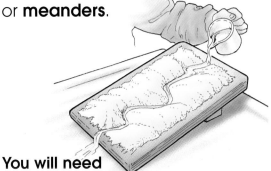

You will need
Some sand, a brick or stone, water in a jug, a large piece of board.

1 Do this outside. Cover the board with sand.

2 Lift one end of the board on to the brick so that it slopes.

3 Trickle water slowly on to the top of the board in one place.

The seashore

If you have been to the seashore, you will know that sea water is salty. Water flows into the sea from rivers. There are many different types of plants and animals in the sea. They all need to stay wet.

Did you know?

Most of the Earth is covered with water. There is ice at the top and bottom of the Earth. Most of the rest of the water is in the seas.

Into the sea

Rivers are made of water. They grow bigger and bigger and sometimes join together. Finally, most of the river water flows into the sea.

Clinging shells

These are limpets. When the tide goes out, they are left on dry rocks. They cling to the rocks, and stay wet inside their shells until the sea returns.

Fish in the sea

All fish need to stay in water because they cannot breathe in the air. Salmon like these sometimes live in the sea and sometimes in rivers.

Now try this

Sea water has salt in it. Salt **dissolves** in water.

You will need
Half a glass of water, a saucepan, a teaspoon of salt, a cooker.

1 Add the salt to the water. Stir it until it disappears.

2 Pour a little salty water into the saucepan. Ask an adult to boil the water until all the water leaves the pan.

3 When the pan is cool, you will see that the salt has been left behind.

Keeping out water

Which clothes do you wear in the rain? Many of our clothes are **waterproof**.

This means that they do not let water through. Do you have waterproof clothes?

Rainy days

On rainy days, we sometimes wear clothes made from waterproof plastic. This girl is wearing a plastic coat and hat, and rubber wellingtons on her feet.

Did you know?

The wet suits that divers wear do not keep out water – they keep water in. The trapped water is warmed by the diver's body, and helps the diver to keep warm in the water.

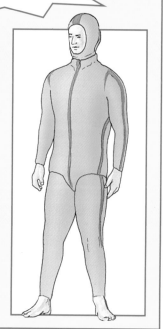

Ducks in water

Ducks spend most of their time in the water. Their feathers need to be waterproof, so that most of their body stays warm and dry.

Duck feathers

Ducks have feathers which are covered in an oily liquid. The oil makes the feathers waterproof because oil and water do not mix.

Now try this

You will need
A jug of water, food colouring, vegetable oil, a drinking glass.

1 Half fill the drinking glass with vegetable oil.

2 Add a few drops of food colouring to the water.

3 Carefully put drops of the water into the oil. The drops will not mix with the oil.

Plants and water

All plants need water. Without it, they die. Some plants live in water. Other plants grow in soil and take up water through their roots.

Did you know?

Pine cones contain seeds. In dry weather the cones open to let the seeds out. Pine cones close up in wet weather.

Underground

Most plants send down long roots into the soil, in search of water. Water from the soil goes up the roots and into the plant. The water carries with it food that the plant needs.

Pond plants

These plants have no trouble finding the water they need because they live in a pond.

Strong roots

Most plants die if they have too much water. These trees are called **mangroves**. Their strong roots keep them out of the water, so they do not get too wet.

Now try this

Without water, seeds cannot grow into plants.

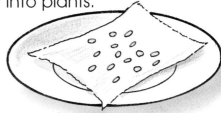

You will need
Two saucers, seeds (mung beans, cress or grass seeds), tissues.

1 Place a tissue on each saucer. Drip a little water on one tissue, to make it damp. Do not put on too much water.

2 Now put about ten seeds on each tissue. Leave the saucers in a light place.

3 Drip water on to the wet saucer every day, but leave the other one dry.

Animals and water

Like plants, all animals need water to live. Some animals, such as whales and fish, live in water. Others live on land but find the water they need in lakes and ponds.

Finding water

Like you, animals need water for drinking and washing. Many animals drink from ponds or lakes. These are often called **watering holes**.

Did you know?

Earthworms spend most of their time underground. But when it rains, they come to the surface so that they do not drown.

Wet skin

Animals such as frogs spend some of their time in the water and some of it on land. We call an animal like this an **amphibian**.

Birds and animals need food and water to live.

You will need
A shallow tray or dish, water, a slice of bread.

1 Put the tray on the ground in the garden or school grounds.

2 Fill the tray with water. Put pieces of bread next to it.

3 Go indoors and watch the tray. After a few days, birds may come to eat the bread and drink the water.

Wet air

There is always water in the air. It is **water vapour**, which is made of water molecules that are too small to see. When the air becomes cold, they join to form drops of water that you can see.

Did you know?

A small town in Chile collects water from the air! Large plastic sheets collect water from fog which forms over the sea daily.

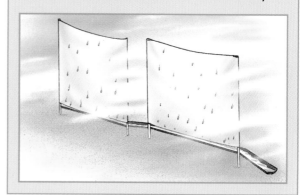

Steam breath

There is water vapour in your breath. On a winter's day, when it is cold, the vapour becomes drops of water which look like steam from a kettle.

Dew drops

Have you ever seen **dew**? You can see it on grass, and on spiders' webs on cold mornings. Dew is tiny drops of water from the air.

Clouds of water

Next time you are in a **mist** or fog, you will know what it is like to be in a cloud. Just like clouds, mist is made of tiny drops of water in the air.

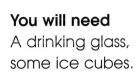
Now try this

When air touches a cold surface, water droplets appear.

You will need
A drinking glass, some ice cubes.

1 Make sure the glass is dry on the inside and on the outside.

2 Put the ice in the glass.

3 Wait for a minute. Now feel the outside of the glass. It is wet.

Getting dry

After a bath or a shower, how do you dry yourself? You probably use a towel. But how does a towel work? What other ways are there to get dry?

Did you know?

After having a bath or a swim you often feel cold, even on a hot day. This is because the water takes away heat when it leaves your skin.

Warm and dry

Clothes dry quickly on a warm, windy day. The water evaporates into the air.

Shaking dry

When dogs are wet, they shake themselves, to get rid of the water. Most people use towels to dry themselves. Towels are made of tiny fibres which soak up the water. A towel can hold lots of water.

Now try this

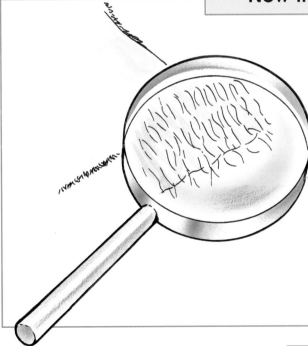

The fibres of a tissue **absorb** water. This means that they soak up the water.

You will need
A tissue, a magnifying glass, a saucer, some water.

1 Tear the tissue in half. With the magnifying glass, look at a torn edge. What can you see?

2 Pour water into the saucer. Touch the water with the edge of the tissue. What happens?

Water in food

What have you eaten today? Do you think the food had water in it? Most foods contain water, but some are dry.

Tomatoes are nearly all water. The water gets into the tomatoes through the roots and stem of the tomato plant.

Wet foods

Our bodies need water. Some of this water comes from the food we eat. Some foods, such as fruit, feel wet. In other foods, such as chocolate, the water is hidden.

Dry foods

Some of the foods we eat are dried so that they can be stored for longer. Milk can be dried to a powder. When the right amount of water is added, the powder becomes milk again.

Now try this

Dry foods stay fresh for longer.

You will need
Two pieces of bread, a plastic bag.

1 Put one piece of bread in a plastic bag. Leave the other one out in a dry place.

2 After a day or so, the bread you left out should be dry – all its water will have been lost.

3 Look at the two pieces of bread each day for the next two weeks.

BE SAFE!
Do not taste the bread when you do this.

In the rain forest

Some of the warmest and wettest places in the world are **rain forests**. Many different types of plants and animals live there.

Did you know?

Because rain forests are so wet, lots of trees grow close together, making the forest dark. Many animals communicate by making loud noises because they cannot see each other.

Warm and wet

The rain forests have so much rain that the ground is soft and damp, and the air is always full of water.

Tree frog

A frog's skin needs to stay wet. The skin of this tree frog can take water from the damp air. It lays its eggs in pools of water in the leaves of rain forest trees.

Now try this

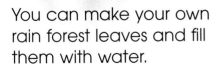

You can make your own rain forest leaves and fill them with water.

You will need
Kitchen foil, a plant sprayer.

1 Make lots of different leaf shapes from the foil.

2 Now spray water on the foil. Do this over a sink or bowl.

3 Water will collect in some parts of the foil. Which shapes are best for collecting water?

Desert plants

The deserts of the world are very dry places. They are very hot during the day.

Desert plants have clever ways of getting water and keeping it.

Desert water

An **oasis** is a part of the desert where water from under the ground comes to the surface. Many plants and animals live in an oasis like the one above.

The water in an oasis often comes from far away, through rocks under the ground.

Waxy surface

A cactus is thick and has a waxy surface. This helps to hold in water. Desert animals often try to eat cactuses for their water. But the cactus has spikes which stop them.

Now try this

Many desert plants have leaves which keep in water.

You will need
A paper bag,
a small plastic bag, two tissues.

1 Fold both tissues in half and drip water on to each one to make them damp.

2 Wrap one tissue in the paper bag. Wrap the other in the plastic bag.

3 Leave the bags somewhere warm. After a few hours, which tissue is still wet?

Desert animals

All animals need water. In the desert, there is very little water. The animals of the desert store water in their bodies, or eat plants or other animals to get water.

Storing water

People can die if they don't drink for a few days. But this camel can go for weeks without drinking water, because it stores water in its hump.

Did you know?

A camel can drink more than 100 litres of water. That is almost enough water to fill a bath.

Seed eater

Like many other small desert animals, gerbils get most of their water from the seeds they eat.

Now try this

You can find water in seeds by crushing them.

You will need
Tissues, black mustard seeds, a wooden spoon.

1 Put some mustard seeds on the tissue.

2 Press the seeds firmly with the wooden spoon to crush them.

3 Lift up the tissue, so the seeds fall off. You should find a little water left behind on the tissue.

Glossary

absorb to soak up a liquid

amphibian an animal which lives on land but whose young live in water

cloud a cloud is made up of many tiny droplets of water

dew tiny drops of water from the air

dissolve to become part of a liquid

evaporate to turn into vapour

ice frozen water

mangrove tropical trees which grow in swamps with their roots above the ground

meander a large bend in a river

mist tiny drops of water in the air

molecule a very small particle, the smallest bit of something

oasis a place in the desert where there is water

rain forest a tropical forest where there is a lot of rainfall

source a place where a stream or river starts

tropics parts of the world where it is hot and wet

watering hole a pool where animals drink and bathe

waterproof something waterproof stops water from getting through

water vapour very small droplets of moisture in the air

Index